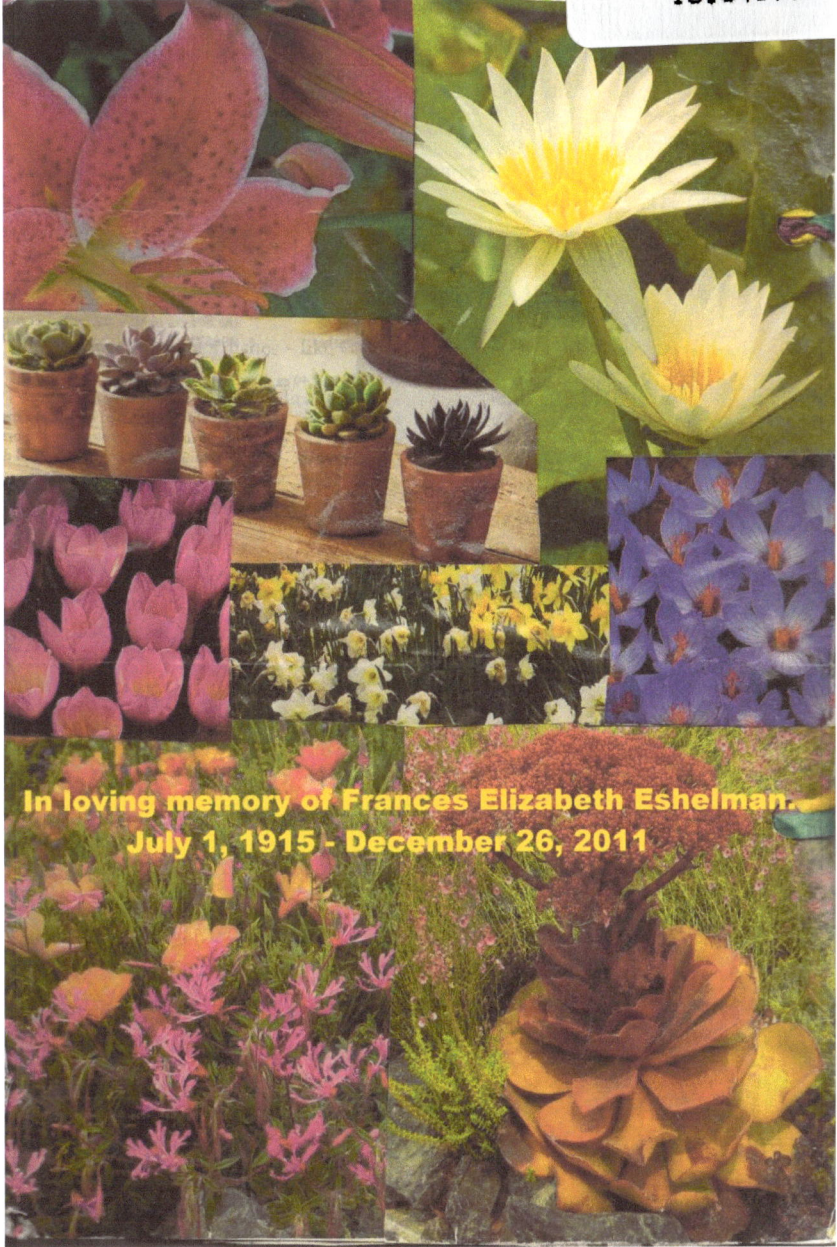

In loving memory of Frances Elizabeth Eshelman.
July 1, 1915 - December 26, 2011

God's Gifts of Healing

The Essentials of LIFE!

by Dr. Jody Evans, ND, CTN, CNHP, D.D.

"Vibraceous, ND"

Essentials of Life Holistic Enrichment Center
214 S. Prospect Avenue
Hartville, Ohio 44632
www.essentials-of-life.org
eolhec@aol.com

God's Gifts of Healing – The Essentials of Life!

ISBN-13: 978-0985450007
ISBN-10: 0985450002

Printed in the United States of America

Dedication

This book is dedicated to my sweet mother,
Frances Elizabeth Eshelman, who introduced me
to natural healing in 1965, and encouraged a
lifelong pursuit of spiritual and healing Truths.
She is the most beautiful woman I know.
She personifies the meaning of
unconditional love.

Thanks, Mom!

xoxo
Love , Jody

Preface

This little book will introduce you to some of God's gifts of healing which were given to all. There are many more. To learn more in depth about these and additional gifts, please read the subsequent books in this series.

Introduction

GOD'S GIFTS OF HEALING... prayer, love, laughter, tears, clean air, light, color, the earth itself, food from the earth (including herbs), pure water, natural fragrance, movement, rest, touch, creativity, sound and many more gifts...

No matter the condition, these things will heal. In combination with one another, they can be used to live a healthier life. Any one of them can be used to bring a person out of sickness and into positive change for the better in health, but it takes the complete combination to achieve our optimal level of health. The more of these gifts we apply, the better the results will be.

Our bodies were divinely designed. In fact, we were created in the image and likeness of God! The planet upon which we live was also perfectly made. Earth was perfectly made to support life on Earth, providing us with all that we need.

Everything has been here since the beginning of time that we need to stay healthy and well. We don't have to invent anything to live healthy lives! Modern technology should be used only for the sake of convenience. It should be like a servant, not the master of us.

We should apply our efforts towards learning ways of applying nature to better our lives, instead of always trying to make something "better" than that which is already perfect. If nature didn't work to our benefit, then surely we'd be extinct! We need to trust in the wisdom of God if we are to make full use of our healing gifts. Let's take a closer look at a few of these gifts, one by one:

PRAYER
LOVE
LAUGHTER
TEARS
AIR
LIGHT
COLOR
EARTH
FOOD
HERBS
WATER
AROMA
MOVEMENT
REST
TOUCH
CREATIVITY
SOUND

PRAYER

Prayer is the conscious path to connecting our mind with the Infinite Mind of God. If we use affirmative prayer -- affirming our Oneness with the Perfect Design of the Universe -- we begin to express that perfection in us. This is healing. The more steadfastly we cling to this connection and refuse to allow the misconception of negative thinking to enter our conscious mind, the more our body will conform to the idea of perfection that is planted within.

We were created in the image of God...in the image of Perfect Life. We are meant to be clear, open channels for the Goodness of God to work through. This is the example Christ Jesus set, and we were all invited to follow Him.

We don't have to beg God to heal us. It is God's will for us to be well. What we must do during prayer is to turn our will over to God. "Thy will, not my will, be done."

God sees us as perfect and whole. When we can see ourselves in this way, our health is free to take form through our faith.

Negative thinking shows a great lack of faith. Instead of bringing forth good, substance takes form as that which we do not desire, if this is where our attention is fixed. This is prayer in reverse. Our beliefs manifest themselves through our thoughts. "Whatever ye shall ask in prayer *believing*, ye shall receive." *(Matthew 21:22)*

When we steady our mind on the perfection of God working through us and take peace in knowing that health is at the core of our being, then we open the door to true healing. "As a man thinketh within his heart, so is he." *(Proverbs 23: 7)*

The false belief that we can be separate from good, is to believe we are separated from God. This is erroneous thinking, and it is the source of all sickness, pain and lack in our life. When we envision ourselves to be separate from Infinite Good (God), we cut ourselves off from our Source and our health is compromised.

Become as a little child when you pray.

Children believe with all of their hearts...that's what we need to do if we're to be healed!

So even when you don't feel very well, affirm that God's health and vitality are within every cell of your being, energizing you and making you well.

Let nothing deter you from this belief. God's strength IN YOU is making you strong!

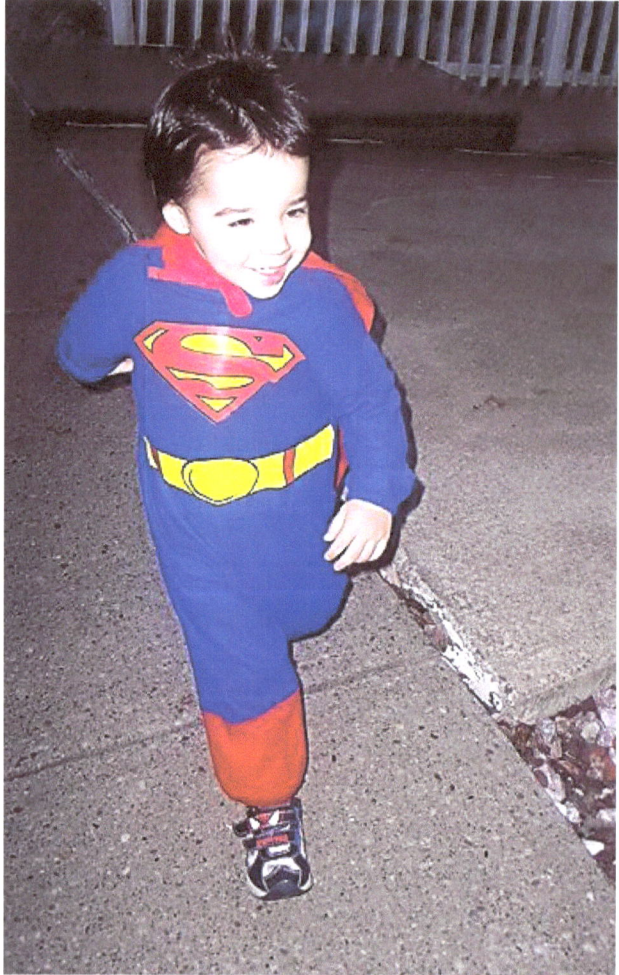

True prayer is the conscious realization of the constant presence of God in our life. God the Good in our life. Omnipotent, Omnipresent, Omniscient. All-powerful, everywhere present, all-knowing God, working in and through our life for good. There's not a spot where God is not! Look for the Good, it is there.

It is the thoughts, words and actions which we express in our day to day lives which constitute what we believe. This is where faith comes into prayer--We have to have faith to believe that God (Good) is at work in our life even when things don't look good to us. It is this belief that grants us the grace to successfully pray and be healed.

Give thanks that you always have what you need to radiate God's perfect health. Pray for guidance and willingness to use what has been given, and then ACT on God's guidance, for faith without works is dead! Proper guidance will come if you ask. Knock and the door is opened to you.

Pray for others, as well, for in praying sincerely for them, you are healed.

In particular, pray for those who have hurt you or for whatever reasons you harbor resentments against. Forgiveness of others (and of yourself!) is essential to radiant health.

Sickness is a diversion from perfect design. We were designed to be well. We were also designed in the image and likeness of God. God is Love. To hold unforgiveness within our heart is to hold ourselves separate from love...to hold ourselves separate from God. God can heal all sicknesses for God is Infinite Life...the Source and the Substance of all. To hold ourselves separate from God is to hold ourselves separate from the Life Force itself.

Prayer is the connecting link.

LOVE

Love is the greatest healer of all, for God IS Love, and any time Love is expressed, it brings us closer to God... whether acknowledged as such or not.

No true and complete healing can ever occur until forgiveness and love are held in the heart...for others and for ourselves.

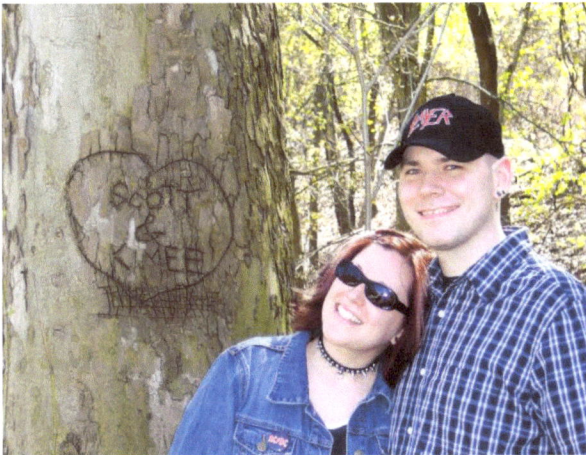

Talking to a friend, spending time with family and loved ones, doing something to help someone else...these are all important to health. Allowing others to care for us is good, too, as is taking good care of ourselves. These are all expressions of love.

Studies have shown that people who spend time with others tend to enjoy a greater degree of good health in their lives.

Even loving a pet can make us feel better. Love truly does heal all wounds! Love for God, for others, and for ourselves...

Unconditional love.

Loving God means loving what God has given to us. It means trusting that God is healing us now. It means to celebrate life! It means living our lives in abundant grace.

To disgrace God by defiling nature is not showing love, nor is to believe it is necessary out of a sense of lack. For if we believe that God will provide for our needs, then surely there are better ways. Loving God means learning and using those ways.

Loving others means to love everyone. Even love those who have done us wrong. Forgiveness is essential to healing. It is easy to love the people (and creatures) we like, but to love those we dislike as well is a powerful healer, indeed.

Loving others means to love them for who they are, and not curse them for not being who we think they should be.

To love ourselves means to send love to every cell of our being. It means forgiving ourselves and believing we are worthy of the absolute best. Loving ourselves means understanding that we are all children of God, created in the image and likeness of Love, Goodness, Intelligence, Beauty and Perfect Life!. It means thinking of ourselves as nothing less.

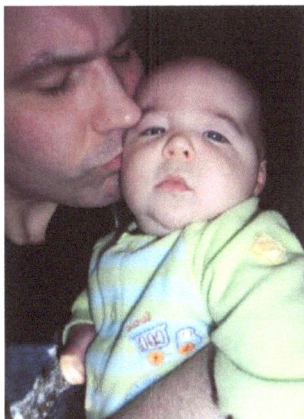

We often think of love as a feeling, but it goes much deeper than that. When love is merely a feeling, it is quite selfish, indeed, because it only serves to make us feel good and does not consider the other individual involved. This is not truly love.

Love instead is a verb. It requires action to be complete.

So in order to love thy God, it is important to show it through the actions you take. USE what God has so graciously provided for you, and rejoice in the goodness of life, knowing that all of your needs are being met! Live in accordance with God's natural and spiritual laws.

To love others, instead of just feeling the love, bring it to life...DO something to help raise them up!! Express it directly or indirectly, but don't keep it locked up in your heart.

The same thing goes for giving love to yourself. Take good care of yourself! Take action in the interest of your health every day. Don't put yourself last on the list! You're worth the time, the money and the effort it takes to live as well as you possibly can!

LAUGHTER

Laughter brings joy and humility-- Joy is expansive and humility contracts. Balance is achieved in this way. Allow the mind and body to follow the spirit of joy and humility, and healing occurs.

Laughter has been shown in studies to increase immune power and even helps prevent heart disease. It is true!

Laughter affects the physical body in many ways, because it changes our brain chemistry in a positive manner. Just the mere act of smiling causes muscles to massage certain parts of the brain which prompt us to feel good all over. Big deep belly laughs massage internal organs, as well.

Laughter is also a good pain reliever. I laughed all through labor and childbirth! It's true!

Most importantly, laughter allows us to let down our guard in order that we can let go and let God. The path to healing is much quicker and more direct then. (We otherwise just tend to get in the way!)

Laughter is very relaxing and invigorating all at the very same time. So, laugh at life's follies! Taking life too seriously leads to worrying, and worrying leads to no good. God is in charge, we are not, so let go and let God and just LAUGH! Laughter truly is the best medicine of all!

TEARS

Tears release stress, pain, guilt, anger, frustration and fear. They cleanse us of negative emotions which keep us sick. Toxic chemicals are actually released through our tears.

Tears also bring humility to us. Humility indicates a submission to God. It is when we let go and let God that we're healed. God is the presence of Life itself. It's necessary to surrender to win. Good health is God's perfect health expressing through us, which is according to Perfect Design. Tears release everything that is not part of the Plan. It really does help to cry!

God hears our cries always, and heals us through our very tears, if we allow ourselves the leisure to cry.

Should tears become overwhelming, any number of God gifts can help bring you around, such as prayer, love, laughter, touch, sunshine, aromatherapy, flower essences, herbs, rest, meditation, exercise, color healing, music or one of the creative arts. And of course, remember to breeeeathe...

AIR

Breath is Life. With every inhale we breathe in the precious gift of life, and each time we exhale, we breathe poisons out. In with the good, out with the bad, so the old saying goes. It is true! It is important to breathe in and out -- deeply, slowly, calmly, completely. In with the good and out with the bad.

Our body takes in vital energy and releases that which we no longer need. We are in perfect concert with all of life in this process...a symbiotic relationship with the plant life. Everything living needs air.

Breathe deeply and slowly and be aware of the presence of God in every breath that you take. Breathe out all the toxins, bad feelings and fears.

It's easy to take the process of breathing for granted, but every cell of our body needs adequate oxygen supplies for us to stay healthy and well. Every cell also needs to be cleansed of toxins, many of which we exhale every time we breathe out.

Breathe in all the way to your belly and breathe out as much as you can. Let your lungs fill back up normally, and know with each breath you are well.

Try breathing in for the count of 8, then hold it until the count of 8, and then breathe out for the entire count of 8 again. In through the nose, and out through the mouth. (You may need to work your way up. If you become dizzy, reduce the number of counts.) There are numerous other breathing techniques designed to strengthen your lungs...alternate nostril breathing technique, and many more. Practice breathing exercises each and every day to live a longer and healthier life!

Fresh air should be obtained for at *least* 15 minutes each day, even during the winter months. Open the window and put your head out if you don't feel like walking outside. It's important to breathe in good fresh outdoor air every day! Indoor air quality should be checked. Be sure to have your air ducts regularly cleaned and ensure adequate ventilation. It's good to open the windows each morning to air the house out, at least for a bit.

Growing houseplants is another good way to help improve the quality of the air in your home. They put out oxygen and take in carbon dioxide. They make perfect companions for us!

Plant essences (essential oils) are also good to spray in the air. They work to clean the air and replace toxins with helpful aromas to promote good respiratory function and otherwise improve our health. Spraying artificial chemicals into the air is one of the worst things you can do. Think of what you're breathing in!

Cancer, heart disease, high blood pressure, asthma, anxiety...Virtually every disease is either caused by or worsened by poor oxygen supply or to synthetic chemicals breathed in.

Do what you can to improve your breathing function each day, and not only will you add years to your life, but life to your years! Increased vitality, stamina and improved health will be the results.

SUNLIGHT

Sunlight brings energy down to the earth! It lends its rays to our eyes, to our skin, to make colors, and to the plants that we eat. It keeps us warm and it gives us our Vitamin D in a natural way, which is always the very best way.

The whole planet energizes itself during the day. During the night it hides from our view so we can sleep, which is equally as important, but the sunshine brings happy days! Light enters the eye and stimulates the pineal gland. This is said to be the seat of the soul by some, and it is widely known as the master gland of the body, as well.

We need sunshine each and every day, even if it's snowing or raining outside. Go to the window if nothing else, and bask for a few minutes there! But when you can, do yourself the best favor, and go out into the sun a wee bit each day. Not too much, but a little is like plugging into the recharger. The sun is crucial to all life on earth. Without it we'd wither and die. Soak up the sun's healing rays! At least 15 minutes each day is good, even if there are clouds.

When you simply can't get enough sun, try some full-spectrum lighting. Full-spectrum lighting has the full spectrum of rays that emit from the sun. This is important because of the particular kind of energy each ray conveys. Each wave length is different in its healing power. Color is interpreted by the brain like a code. Color comes from the sun as a gift in itself.

COLOR

Ohhhhhhhhhhhh, how often we forget about color in our quest for healing, and how easy it is to apply! God gave us such an incredible array of beautiful colors, and each one carries its own special and healing vibrational pattern.

Nature is all full of color...green, blue, red, yellow, purple, pink, orange and every variation of color between. The sky, the foliage, the beautiful colors of flowers and birds...there is so much magnificent color everywhere to be seen.

Color is a magnificent healer! Each color has a different frequency, which affects what it has to offer to us. This is all part of God's Perfect Plan!

Colorful flowers, the colors that make up the sky, the green of the vegetation, the colors of precious gems and the vibrant colors of the ocean and everything living therein...they all can affect us in positive ways!

Blues are relaxing while oranges are energetic...each color brings its own gifts. Make your wardrobe and your surroundings reflect the colors you need.

The color of food gives clues to the nutrients that it contains. The colors should be vibrant and varied to make a good diet. Dark greens, light greens, oranges and reds... yellows and purples and blues...our food comes from the earth and carries the vibrations of life.

Each color in food indicates a different nutritional composition. A well-balanced meal has a well-balanced color scheme! Too often people have plates that show nothing but all whites and browns.

Colors can be used in so many ways, such as in creative endeavors, the clothes we adorn, the color of our décor.

A garden can add beautiful color, as can the birds and the butterflies that it attracts!

Color therapy is known as Chromotherapy, and has been in use since ancient times. Great halls were constructed where people would come to be bathed in light filtered through panes of glass of various colors for the purpose of healing. Healers still use this and other similar techniques today.

Using colors in healing works on deeper levels of the spirit and mind, making it easier for the body to heal. The body is programmed to recognize color through its vibrations as a healing code.

Imagining various colors while meditating or performing massage also has profound healing effects, adding the power of relaxation to benefit more.

In healing with gems, colors give their special energy amplified directly from the earth through the stones.

Gem healing is very powerful, because these are the pure colors given to us from the earth. Each stone carries vibrations specific to its precise color and mineral composition, and these correspond directly to vibrations in us. Crystals, amethysts, emeralds and even fool's gold have their purpose in healing. It's all part of God's perfect plan.

White is commonly thought of as having no color at all, but actually, it is all colors combined in perfect balance. White is very effective in healing, because it brings harmony. It is a common practice in prayer circles and amongst healers to imagine a person surrounded by white healing light. This is a way to protect someone in prayer. Imagine them surrounded by white holy light, protecting them and keeping them safe at all times. Inside the circle of white is their own energy field. See healing colors in your mind's eye during prayer.

What color is your energy field? Hold a clear image of strong, vibrant colors fast in your mind, and you will begin to radiate healing energy now!

WATER

Water is life's great replenisher. It is essential to every function of the whole entire body, as it is to the entire physical world. It is as important to life as is the air that we breathe.

Only 48 ounces of water is needed to keep the body functioning each day. While this is true, it takes quite a bit more to keep the body running at its absolute best. Is our aim to simply survive or is it to experience optimal health? A good rule of thumb is to divide your body weight by two and then drink than number of ounces spread over the course of the day.

While it is true that much of the water content we need is derived from our food, over time it taxes the body to draw most of its water from foods. Much of the water in foods is used up in the digestive process, while there is no effort to digesting water alone.

It is very important that water be free from impurities, including unhealthy microorganisms, chemical pollution and added fluoride. Buy a water filter or else be the filter yourself, placing an extra burden on your kidneys and liver.

Drinking distilled water is the best way to make sure your water is totally pure. While it is true that distilled water no longer contains the natural minerals that occur in nature, it is still the best choice for drinking because it is not only free from impurities, but it also works to pull toxins and heavy metals out of the body like no other water is able to do.

Whatever form of water you drink, remember that you can filter your water before drinking it, or after drinking it...your choice. It's easier on your kidneys to filter before!

Municipal water sources are not refined enough to sift everything out in today's chemical world, leaving most public waters polluted to some extent, not to mention the controversy regarding the addition of fluoride to our water supply, when there are known links to health problems from this.

The most important consideration, however, is that we DRINK PLENTY OF WATER! If you don't, you will gradually wither and die!

The effects of dehydration are often given the name of a disease and some kind of drug to supposedly cure it, but water is the only cure for such conditions.

Hardening of arteries and every organ occurs when we don't take in enough pure water to drink. Many illnesses can result from this. We're even told that some of these illnesses don't have a cure, but others will tell you that water's the cure.

Every cell of the body is bathed in water. There is water inside each cell and between every cell. It is by far the bulk of our mass.

When the body does not receive enough water, it will manifest symptoms to protect itself. For instance, high cholesterol is the body's attempt at protecting the brain and the nerves from the effects of dehydration. To take drugs to lower the cholesterol without addressing the issue of dehydration can have serious side effects on the body. This is true of high blood pressure or any situation regarding a need for water. Drugs do not satisfy this basic need, but merely mask the prevailing symptoms through artificial means. Water must be increased for any real change to be made.

Water has also been used for healing throughout time in the form of baths. More water enters into your system at bath time than you could possibly drink in a day! For purposes of healing, do not add any synthetic ingredients to the bath water or use chemical bath products. Essential oils, mineral salts, herbs and other pure natural additives are a soothing and healing enhancement to bath water. Synthetic chemicals and fragrances are not.

EARTH

It is important to feel connected to our Mother Earth. Too many people never come into contact with the ground upon which we all live. We need to be grounded to be truly well.

The earth has a polarity, and so do we. We are electro-magnetic beings in our earthly expression, with north and south poles just like the earth. With all of the technology in today's world, our signals get scrambled, so to speak. It is important to realign ourselves with the earth's energy field, in order for inner balance to be achieved. Try walking barefoot out in the woods, laying on your lawn or hugging a tree! This will greatly help in feeling more relaxed and re-energized.

The earth is full of magnetic minerals and so are we. In the beginning, we had no shoes, and the strength of the earth transferred to us through our feet as we walked, giving us strength, extending the earth's power through us.

The daily medicine from the herbs entered our bloodstream, as well, as we walked barefoot, to keep us healthy and strong. We were meant to walk on the earth, but how often do any of us go outside without shoes?

Our food gains its mineral content from what's in the soil. If you grow food in soil that's depleted, it will not contain the same nutrients as what you will find in food grown in rich, naturally mineralized soil. If the minerals aren't in the soil, they won't be in the food. That is unless they're added in, but these are not assimilated in the body the same.

This is one reason why it is so important to eat sustainably grown organic foods. Become acquainted with the farming methods of your food supply! Most commercially grown food is not grown in this way. Check your area for sources of locally grown organic food. The nutritional value of food is greatly dependent upon how it is produced. Make sure it's produced naturally from good healthy earth.

FOOD from the Earth (including HERBS)

"And God said, Behold, I have given you every herb bearing seed, which is upon the face of all the earth, and every tree, in the which is the fruit of a tree yielding seed; to you it shall be for meat. And to every beast of the earth, and to every fowl of the air, and to everything that creepeth upon the earth, wherein there is life, I have given every green herb for meat: and it was so." *(Genesis 1:29-30)*

God gave us plants as our food--and the fruit and the seeds and the nuts and the herbs. Plants give us exactly what we need from the earth to survive. They nourish our bodies completely to stay healthy and overcome all disease. Our physical sustenance comes from the earth. A plant-based diet is best.

When we eat, it should not be simply to fill our bellies, but rather to nourish, cleanse, balance and strengthen our bodies. In a good diet, every single bite should count towards our health.

Food should be eaten as closely as possible to the way it was given to us, because this is when it's in perfect form -- whole, raw, in-season, locally grown, without poisonous chemicals and without being overly processed.

Food is supposed to give Life, so it must contain the Life Force it gives. Processed foods simply cannot offer to us what we need. Fake foods clog up the system and do a great deal of harm.

NATURAL FOODS are REAL and they promote NATURAL HEALTH! Artificial means fake, and artificial foods promote sickness.

Pesticides, hormones, steroids, antibiotics, synthetic fertilizers, chemicals, genetically modified organisms, irradiated foods, foods shipped hundreds and even thousands of miles, foods chemically ripened, processed and refined foods, artificial colors, flavors, sweeteners and preservatives, foods produced through factory farming, foods

which have been enriched with synthetic vitamins and inorganic minerals and then microwaved, fried, charbroiled, or in some other way completely destroyed...these things are not fit to eat. These types of food have no life energy left in them to give.

When eating food in its natural state, such as raw fruit and veggies, sprouted grains, raw nuts and seeds, natural sweeteners, and other raw natural foods which have been locally, organically and sustainably grown, you are doing the best for your body that you possibly can.. All of the plant's nutrition comes in exactly the right proportions in this type of food, and it is completely bio-available to us.

Vitamins, minerals, enzymes, essential fatty acids, glyconutrients, antioxidants, amino acids, good fats, complex carbohydrates, complete proteins...These all come from a balanced diet of natural foods.

When you cook food, you should supplement your diet with food enzymes and other plant-based nutrients, because cooking will destroy most of the enzymes and nutritional value. Be sure the supplements you use are plant-based and of good quality.

Drinking fresh juices can greatly expedite the process of healing because they deliver such concentrated nutrients to us. Green smoothies and such are great for added nutrition, but for the fastest therapeutic benefits that you can get from food, juicing is the ideal way. It is a very good practice to drink at least 16 ounces of fresh raw juice

every day, especially if you're targeting a particular need. This will be covered in further detail in subsequent books in this series.

Vegetables and fruits are alkalinizing to the system, whereas nuts, grains, dairy products and meats are acid forming. Fats are neutral on the pH scale and are therefore helpful in neutralizing over acidifying foods. For good health, a diet should consist of about 80% alkalizing foods. This can easily be monitored with an old-fashioned pH strip with the first morning urine each day.

Fruits are the most cleansing foods, while vegetables are the most healing. Proteins are your builders, of course, and fats serve to lubricate the body, which is extremely important...IF they are raw and natural, i.e., virgin, expeller- or cold-pressed oils. Otherwise, it's extremely close chemically to eating plastic!

When making salad dressings, make the dressing a contributing part of your meal, as well as any other dressings, sauces and condiments you use.

Fats are a very necessary part of a good diet. Coconuts, avocados and raw nuts are very good sources of fats. Seeds, such as flax seed or hemp seed and their oils are excellent, too.

Adding natural fats to the diet will keep the body from craving bad fats. Supply the need and the craving will go. The same thing holds true with sugars, salts, and other food cravings—the real deal will satisfy the urge like no amount of diet pills can.

Sugars should be natural, such as stevia leaves, raw agave, dates and other fruits. Refined white processed sugar is stripped of its nutrients and makes blood sugar plummet and soar, while artificial sweeteners are literally poison to us. Natural sweeteners, on the other hand, enhance health. This should be the guiding rule with whatever you eat.

As for salt, we should be getting our sodium from foods like celery and asparagus. Table salt and salt added to processed foods causes problems with the balance of fluids within the body and ruins our taste buds for natural tastes. Herbs make good seasoning agents, and should be a mainstay in any good diet. They are very important to health.

Herbs are food, too. Many herbs can be used as medicine, and are extremely effective as such. Overall, however, herbs work to nourish the body to do the healing itself.

Herbs are not at all the same things as drugs. Herbs are alive with the energy of LIFE. They are perfectly suited to give the body the elements it needs in the perfect delivery system to help it function as it normally should. Herbs work to cleanse, balance and nourish the body to health.

Drugs are lifeless and therefore incapable of supplying life to the body. This is why you will find in the United States that we spend less money on food than any country, but we're first place in medical bills! We should be paying more attention to the healing powers of herbs and other foods.

The best way to use herbs is to eat them raw, or to drink them infused into a tea. Herbal medicines can also be directly applied or made into a tincture or an elixir. Taking herbs in capsules is very convenient, but if taste is part of the delivery system, as is the case with many digestive herbs, then this aspect of the herb is lost when a capsule is used.

There is very little danger in using herbs by themselves, but when using prescription or over-the-counter medications at the same time, it is best to seek the advice of a qualified practitioner. Nothing in this booklet is intended to take the place of a doctor's advice. It is simply being suggested that herbs can meet some of your nutritional needs and help cleanse, balance and nourish your body so it can heal itself, as was intended by God when first placed on this earth for our use in this way.

If herbal supplements are purchased commercially, be sure of your source. Many herbs on the market are lifeless, cheap, adulterated with chemical additives, or grown with synthetic fertilizers and pesticides used. The very best herbs are the ones which grow naturally right under your feet. But if you purchase your herbs, know the source and their practices.

It matters a great deal under what kind of conditions herbs are grown, harvested, stored, transported, formulated, processed and packaged. Most herbs are safe that grow right under your feet, and most are safe from reputable dealers. The main concern with your source is lack of potency, though, and whether they're truly all natural or not. You'd be surprised how many are not. Regulation is not the answer. Doing your own research is.

NATURAL FRAGRANCE

Nature provides the most wonderful scents! Flowers, fruits, the sweet smell of the air after a rain...These are all very good to breathe in! They bring healing gifts not just to the mind, but to the body, as well!

The essence of the plant is contained in the scent, and passed onto us through our nose. These natural essences have characteristics such as being antibacterial, antifungal, mood enhancing, and much, much more. These essences can be applied to just about any condition we may find ourselves in. Aromatherapy is a study unto itself. God had a marvelous plan!

The nasal passageway into the body (olfactory system) runs through the brain, and the elements of the fragrance are sent throughout our body from there. Every system of the body can be positively affected through natural aromas, such as our respiratory, circulatory, endocrine, digestive and nervous systems.

The olfactory pathway runs particularly close to where the limbic system resides. The limbic system is the more primitive part of the brain. It is linked to emotion, memory, sex drive and intuition. The limbic system also controls heart rate, breathing rate, blood pressure and stress levels.

The hypothalamus is a part of the limbic system. The hypothalamus controls the pituitary gland, which controls the entire endocrine system. Metabolism, growth and development, tissue function, and sexual function are all governed there and affected by scent.

While natural fragrances have a very positive effect on our functions, it is important to realize that synthetic fragrances have just as profound effect in a negative way. Synthetic fragrances are very detrimental to the nervous system, the sinuses, and the lungs, and the endocrine system. They travel through the same channels and impact the same parts of the brain. They are not only irritating, but extremely toxic for us to breathe in. This is alarming considering the amount of synthetic fragrances we are exposed to in everyday life. It's a very acceptable practice and yet so dangerous.

Hair sprays, deodorants, lotions, perfumes -- all meant to beautify -- actually make people sick. Asthma, cancer, nervous conditions, migraines and even birth defects have been linked to synthetic aromas. Look for the label to specify 100% essential oils, or you can easily make your own natural products yourself with common ingredients and essential oils.

Natural fragrances are genuinely uplifting, to yourself and to others. They are extremely attractive; true aphrodisiacs indeed. And they are antibacterial, too, making them so many uses in bath and beauty products and in the home.

Cleaning products, designed to make our environment more beautiful and sanitary, but today's commercial cleaners are actually polluting the air and leaving a toxic film on the surfaces we clean. We shouldn't have to clean after cleaning!

Natural essential oils used in these products not only do a far better job in sanitizing the air and the surface of things, but they also leave a beautiful scent in the air which is healthy to breathe. They actually work to clean our bodies inside whenever we breathe them in, instead of damaging our tissues and making us ill.

When going for a walk in the woods, breathe in the fresh scent of pine and realize that it is cleaning your lungs just the way pine cleaners work at cleaning your floor!

Lavender is very soothing and is good for pain, nervousness, and many more things. Applied directly it is very good for rashes, itches, sores, burns and other things which need soothed. Plus it has a fabulous smell!

Citrus oils are very uplifting. Frankincense is good for tissue repair and also the lungs. Peppermint is good for colds, sinus problems, digestion and memory. All of the oils are good for so many things! Most are antibacterial, antiviral, antifungal, and antimicrobial, among other things. It is well worth your time to study these oils and use them in your daily life, not only as alternatives to synthetically fragranced products, but as an enhancement to health.

MOVEMENT

Everything in all of life moves. Movement is within our being right down to our cells. It is healthy to keep our blood flowing, our heart beating, our lymphatic system pumping away. Rocking, walking, running, swaying, jumping, dancing, stretching, spinning, moving back and forth, to and fro, up and down.

Movement is important for how our body functions and for the way that we feel. It is important that movement be in accordance with our design, and be part of our everyday life. Movement should be something we naturally do if we're to be healthy.

So find what feels right for you, and stretch yourself as far as you comfortably can. It's actually more uncomfortable in the long run to *not* exercise, because if stiffness and achy joints set in, there's nothing comfortable about even getting out of your chair! So move now so you can move more easily later. The effects are accumulative.

The easiest way to begin is to just move every part of your body. Wiggle your fingers, your toes, move your eyes all around...move everything you have every way it will go, and see what your body can do. Move this way and that...always stretch in both directions for balance. Not just this way...but this way and that! Professional training is good to use, but you can do a lot on your own.

Think about what you are feeling...become familiar with your body's responses. Think about the organs inside that are also being massaged as you stretch. Tell your whole body it is healthy and well...down to each little cell.

Incorporate movement into your everyday life. Think about how you walk, when you walk, how far you walk. Do you ever run, jog, dance, skip, reach, climb, bicycle, exercise, do yoga, or sway???

Be sure and move enough to let your body know you're alive!!!

Stretching yourself is key. Start where you are. Don't expect more of yourself than you are *able* to do, but at the same time, you must realize that you are capable of more than you think. So do more than you *think* you can do!

If you can wiggle your toes, then try to stretch them back, and then move on to rotating your feet around and around. Start at this basic level to increase body awareness.

Work your way up to moving the trunk of your body and twisting and stretching. Don't stop until you get to the top of your head. Move to your limit and then push yourself a little bit more. It will do your whole body, mind and spirit such good!

Take up active hobbies.

Move yourself in your thinking, too. Be open-minded. Get out of your comfort zone. Don't allow stagnation to set in. Do puzzles, change your routine, read, listen to other points of views besides your own. Try to learn something new every day!

KEEP MOVING! Don't stay stuck in one spot!

REST

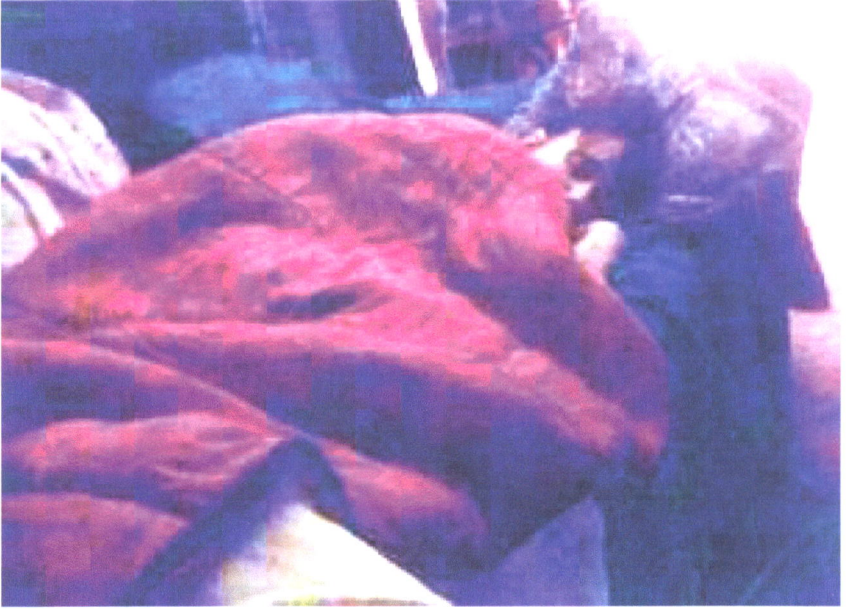

Just as important as movement is rest. When the body and the mind are at rest, the spirit is receptive to commune freely with God. This is that place of perfect peace. "Be still and know I am God." This is when we receive comfort and healing insight.

The body heals while it is resting. The stages of deep sleep are especially important. This is the time when we dream, discharging off old emotions, and gaining insight to our subconscious mind. This is also when we are in touch with the astral realm. Delta brain waves are experienced when we are in the deep stages of sleep. This is when much regeneration and healing occurs.

Sleep should be regular, and uninterrupted, if possible...and it should be in the dark. Take the few moments before falling asleep to speak healing words of peace and relaxation to all of your body parts. This will promote deeper sleep.

There are many herbal, homeopathic, and aromatherapy natural sleep aids you can use which are very safe and promote natural sleep, as can lullabies, prayers and someone to love. All of these are better alternatives than drugs.

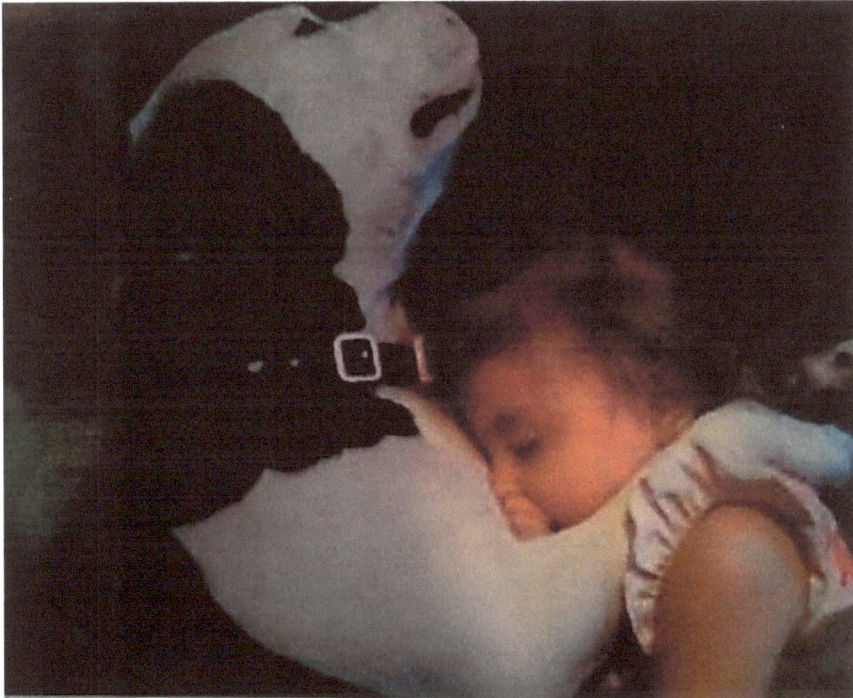

Sleep is a natural thing! It should come about by natural means.

Over-the-counter drugs, prescription medication and alcohol may cause you to fall asleep, but they do not promote healthy sleep patterns. It's best to avoid the side effects these types of substances carry with them. There is not one single chemical drug in existence that does not carry negative side effects. Some of these adverse reactions can be quite serious. Some can be deadly, in fact.

Meditation and other forms of deep relaxation can also provide the body and mind with a safe way to relax. The state of mind that is experienced in meditation is that of being completely relaxed but awake. This state is extremely important as well. The brain waves in this state are called theta waves. Our mind is very open to suggestion while in this state, and it is a perfect time to repeat affirmations and speak words of healing to every cell of our being.

This is the state to be in for guided or self-hypnosis, as well as meditation.

Wandering thoughts can easily be brushed aside in order to empty the mind of all worry. Simply be still in the Silence and listen for the guidance which comes from within. This is when God speaks most directly to us. Ask a question when deeply relaxed and the answer will immediately come.

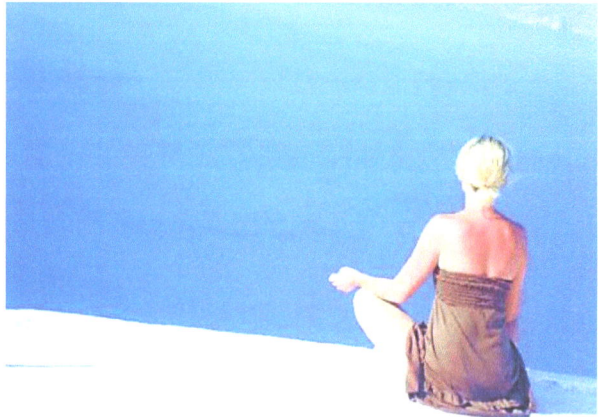

Meditative states of mind are not only restful to the mind but also the body. The body heals, as pointed out, during sleep, but it also heals during these conscious states of relaxation, too. Meditation lowers our blood pressure, slows our breathing, decreases our heart rate, increases our immune power, and releases physical tension from our bodies.

Alpha brain waves occur when the brain is in a more active state than when theta or delta occur, but it is still a very relaxed state of mind. This state of mind can be achieved throughout the day while awake, imparting a very peaceful feeling which allows us to function with clarity.

The more time one spends in meditation, the easier it becomes to control these states of mind and not give into the incessant chatter that can take our peace.

To take a few minutes each day to rest the body and mind...in meditation...in a nap...in an activity that is restful and refreshing to you...will help in so many ways to get through the rest of the day.

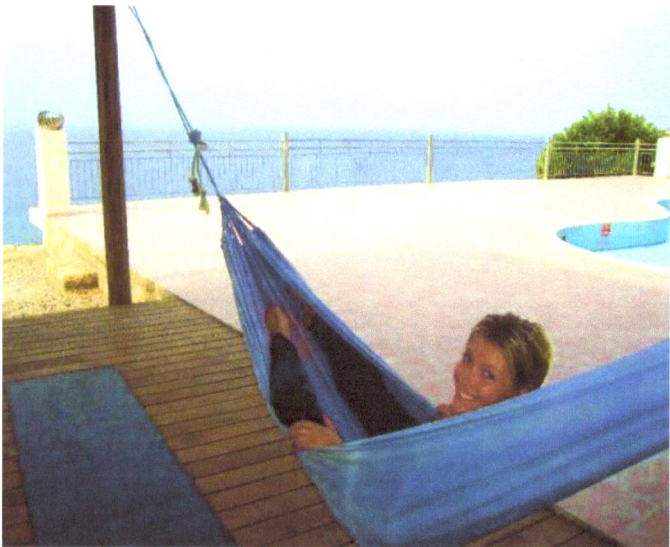

Resting the mind by taking time away from daily responsibilities and cares is important. It is easy to think there is no time to relax, but relaxing from time to time makes work hours much more efficient. Many countries shut down the shops so workers can take a nap in the afternoon. Siestas are not a real bad idea, as it turns out!

TOUCH

There is much healing power in touch. A hug; a hand to hold; a pat on the back...God's healing energy flows through the hands to the person in need. Touch is one of our basic needs as an infant, and this need carries on throughout life.

Touch is healing, readily available, and free. So, reach back and rub your neck...rub your feet...rub your hands and your arms and your face and everywhere you can reach!

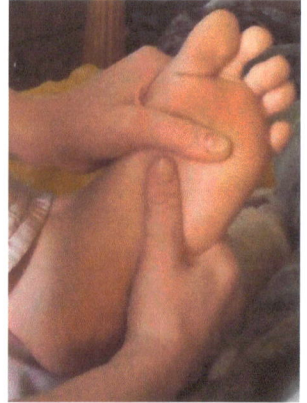

Apply pressure of varying degrees...experiment with the sensation of touch. It is easy to learn reflexology or acupressure, plus just plain relaxing massage is a very good thing.

Massage has been in practice since the beginning of time. It can be specifically applied for therapeutic benefits, or generally applied to promote relaxation. Relaxation in itself is healing, as already discussed. Well nothing relaxes the body and mind quite like a massage!

Use some aromatherapy oil to increase the effectiveness of the treatment you give. Whenever you use these healing gifts in conjunction with one another, it drastically increases the healing power.

Keep in mind that massage releases toxins and pain stored in the muscles. Water will help move these out. Emotions may be released during massage, as well. This is part of the natural healing process for some.

Reflexology is a form of touch healing which involves applying a specific type of touch to various points on the bottoms of the feet, the palms of the hands and/or the ear lobes. These points correspond to various parts of the body, and by stimulating the points, you stimulate healing of that body part, typically organs which cannot be directly reached through massage. It can be used to lessen pain, discomfort and symptoms of disease.

Acupressure is also an ancient healing art involving touch in which pressure is applied to the same points as used in acupuncture all over the body. These points relate to meridian points, and by applying pressure, trapped energy is released and rebalanced, bringing a healing about.

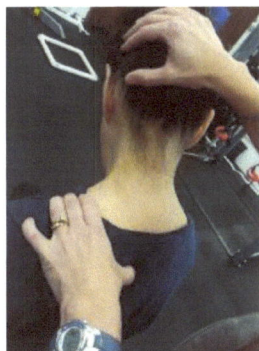

Touch can also be used in such a manner as to stretch the body and release tension in this way, relieving pain. A vast array of structural difficulties can be positively impacted through touch which is skillfully performed.

Be sure the person working with you is qualified. Some forms of touch healing can be safely administered by anyone and carry no risk, but others could be dangerous if improperly applied.

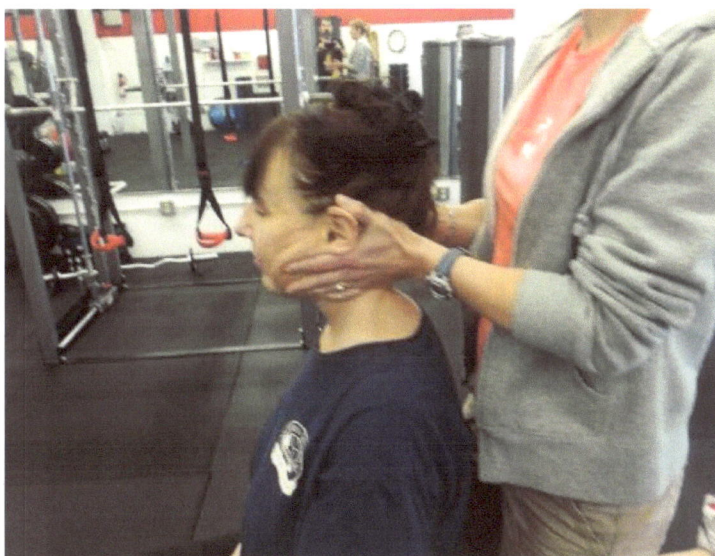

CREATIVITY

Imagination expressed! To create is our birthright, as we were created in the image and likeness of the Creator of all. Great things begin in the imagination...healing is no different from this.

Imagine that you are well. See it fervently in your own mind. Then use your creative powers to make it happen for you, by creating the life that you want! While it is true that it takes the additional effort of doing the work that's required to manifest that which we wish to create, but it is equally as true that all begins in the creative mind.

Creative expression of any kind is great practice for this. Make up a dance, a song, a poem...draw a picture...do some crafts...make up a story...make something from scraps of this and that. Now apply this technique to your health. It is basically the same process for all.

Studies have shown that creativity is good for your health. It helps to relieve stress, for one thing...and stress is at the root of so much disease. Creatively coping with stress can reduce your risk for heart failure, high blood pressure, high blood sugar, depression and so many things.

Creativity also gives rise to self-confidence. To create something is a reminder to us that we can do it. It is empowering to us in so many ways. It opens our mind to possibility thinking. This helps to remove the blocks standing in the way of us getting well.

Engaging in creative activity keeps your mind active! In a sense, it keeps your mind young, always seeking new ways to do things. This has an extremely positive impact upon physical health.

Contact The We Can Make It Group at **eolhec@aol.com** if you're interested in being a part of a group which learns about natural healing through creative endeavor. For more information please visit **www.essentials-of-life.org/WeCanMakeIt.html.**

SOUND

The sound of the sea or the ocean, a babbling brook in the woods, a coyote howling, raindrops and thunder, frogs croaking, crickets chirping, a little bird up in the sky, the rustling of leaves in the wind...Listen to the sounds of the wild. They are such comforting sounds to the ears and the soul. Whether listening to music or making music, the effects are very profound.

It could be the sound of a symphony orchestra, a single instrument, a rock and roll band, or the sound of a human voice. Whatever the source, it is the vibrations which heal us. The vibration of life comes through sound and resonates inside us, making us well.

The rhythm, the beat and the harmony all come into play. To be healing, the music should be harmonious or singular notes, but not full of discord, unless you're trying to release negative energy...but then release it and move into harmonious songs to set the tone for harmonious health. All music has the power to heal.

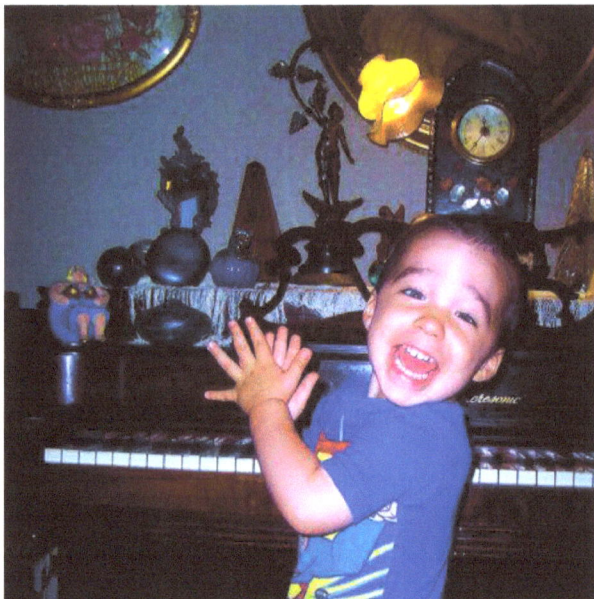

When you use your own voice you add power, so sing! Sing even if you think you don't know how to sing. Breathing exercises can help. If you can breathe, you can sing! Don't only sing when you're happy, but rather sing in order to make yourself happy! It works!

Try karaoke...the word itself is said to translate to mean, "bad singing!" Ha ha! I never thought I would enjoy karaoke, myself, but I have found after trying...I do! Or sing in the shower...or in the car...or while the radio's on. It doesn't matter, just do it and your health will improve...even if only a bit. Singing the song, "Do-Re-Mi," from *The Sound of Music*, three times in a row will bring your whole system in balance, I'm told.

Do voice exercises. Not so much to improve the sound of your voice—although it will—but more to allow each note to impart its own healing power to you. Touch every note...up the scale a few octaves and down. Use every vowel sound...accentuate notes in different ways. Long notes...staccato...experiment with the sound of your voice. Find your own healing song.

The particular words that you sing can also be healing. They can be affirmative...they can lift up your spirits...they can console you...Always be sure your words reflect what you want in your life when you claim them unto yourself, because there is much power in words. Sometimes a lament, the blues or a hard, screaming rock song can be healing, if used to release the pain that is within...but finish up with a nice happy song!

The sound of "Ohhhhmmmm" during meditation stills the mind and brings us closer to God. When using the sound of Ohm, notice how it feels in your body. The vibrations heal so many things.

Some people use tuning forks to bring about healing with sound. Some people use crystal glasses, some may use Tibetan bowls, and still others take part in drum circles.

There are many ways to use sound in healing, and they are all very healing to the mind, body and soul.

The sound of drumming resonates deep within the whole being. Drumming will help get your body in rhythm. Tap on the table if you do not have a drum. Pick up a pair of spoons, rattle some keys, there are so many things around the house that make some kind of sound, so just PLAY!

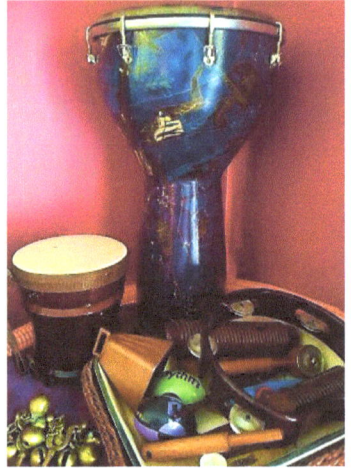

Healing IS fun, and sound healing is one of the most enjoyable forms. So listen to music...make music...listen to the music that nature makes. Bring harmony into your life!

Conclusion

We don't need medical science to invent cures for us. We don't need to use toxic, poisonous drugs which require hideous animal tests. We don't need to give into the idea that we naturally grow weak and sick as we age, or that we inherit disease. What we need to do is to stick to our faith and believe that we were created to be perfect and whole, and we need to use what's been given to us to bring this about.

That's not to say that our bodies are not vulnerable to sickness...they are. We live in a world where we are subjected to toxins and other health inhibiting factors each day, plus birth defects and injuries do occur. Nevertheless, we can learn to live as close as we can to what is truly natural, and enjoy the very best health that we can.

When our life began, a sperm met an egg, and a whole entire body was made, with a soul and a mind planted in. The same Power that made this possible remains active in us throughout life, creating new cells every day to replace the old.

To become decrepit is not a natural part of the ageing process. There are many people who have lived long productive lives past the age of 100. Disease is contrary to our perfect design. It is a sign that something has gone wrong.

God is everywhere present. God is in us. God has been present since the beginning of time. If we are to believe this, then we must believe we can be healed. Just trust and know that God can do all.

It only makes sense that what we need has been with us since the beginning of time, or we wouldn't have survived through the ages. Look to what has been there all along in your search for good health. God created us to be happy and provided us with all that we need.

While it is true that we will not live forever, we should nonetheless set our expectations a little bit higher than we sometimes do...and never, never give up...no matter what doctors or anyone may say. There is no power greater than God, and only God knows what is best. The best was placed in our hands in the beginning and God saw it as good!

Healing comes in many different ways and many different forms. Take comfort in the knowledge that there is nothing which cannot be healed. Turn it over to God by using these gifts and know you have all that you need.

"Look at the birds of the air: they neither sow nor reap nor gather into barns, and yet your heavenly Father feeds them. Are you not of more value than they?" *(Matthew 6:26)*

"I sing because I'm happy...I sing because I'm free! His eye is on the sparrow, and I know He watches me." *(Traditional Hymn by Martin and Gabriel)*

MANY THANKS TO THE FOLLOWING PEOPLE FOR HELP WITH THE PICTURES: Frances Elizabeth Eshelman, Julie Eshelman, Brian Evans, Craig Evans, Dean Evans, Jody Evans, Cora Belle Fegancher, Alyssa Gratz, Kristen Kirtlan, Martha Leighton, Ronny Leighton, Sarah Leighton, Kimee Massie, Maddox Massie, Scott Massie, Jaylan Marie Morris, Tina Walton, Tanya Wells-Eshelman and Danielle Wirick.

Prayer...Makes you receptive to good. God is Good.

Love...it is good...it will make you complete. God is Love.

Laughter...Expresses an inner knowing that all is well.

Tears...Tears release poisons and pains of the body and mind.

Air...The precious breath of life...breathe it in!

Sunlight...Pure energy shining on us.

Color...All the colors radiate with the vibrations of life.

Water...Replenishes life.

Earth...Full of rich minerals to ground us, to balance, to heal.

Food...Let thy food be the medicine and thy medicine be thy food.

Herbs...Herbs are food. Therefore, herbs are medicine.

Natural Fragrance...Good scents make good sense for your health!

Movement...Let your body know you're alive!!!

Rest..."Be still and know I am God."

Touch...God has no hands but ours. Let the healing energy flow.

Creativity ...Opens the mind to the Creator of all.

Song...Establishes harmony within.

"And God saw everything that He had made, and behold, it was very good..." *(Genesis 1:31)*

You are invited to join us to learn more about God's Gifts of Healing by visiting our website--

Essentials of Life

Holistic Enrichment Center

...A Place to Come Together and

GROW!!!

www.essentials-of-life.org

God bless you in your quest for physical, mental and spiritual wellness!

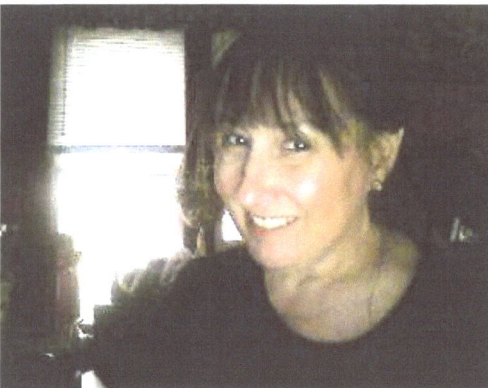

Naturally Yours in Good Health, "Vibraceous, ND"

Dr. Jody Evans, ND, CTN, CNHP, D.D.
Director of Healing Ministries

About the Author...

Mary Jo Evans, ND, CTN, CNHP, D.D.
(Dr. Jody Evans..."*Vibraceous, ND*")

Dr. Evans has been in the study of holistic healing and natural health since the mid-1960's. She earned her Doctor of Naturopathy degree from Trinity College of Natural Health and is recognized by the American Naturopathic Certification Board as a Certified Traditional Naturopath.

Dr. Evans is an ordained Universal Life Church minister, focusing her ministry work on teaching others about God's gifts of healing which have been with us since the beginning of time. She believes there is nothing that cannot be healed through nature and God. It is her sacred mission to teach people to teach people to teach and to work to give folk medicine back to the folks! She founded the Essentials of Life Holistic Enrichment Center to help her in meeting these goals.

www.vibraceous.com

Addendum...

This book is written in the hope that the reader will realize how connected we are to our Source, and how healing really can occur moment to moment, and it really can be easy and fun!

That's what my mother learned when I was staying with her for awhile. I wrote this book at that time, and we used it together as a guide for her healing...for OUR healing, for I used it, too.

She loved reading this book...studying it, in fact...and she gained much comfort and encouragement from what she read. We practiced the principles she was reading about...using aromatherapy oils, singing, saying our prayers, doing our exercises, eating natural foods and keeping our minds and bodies active and alive with Spirit each day...We had a really great time!

At 96 years of age, she was off all medications, and living a fulfilling life with her family in spite of her age and the many challenges she had. She was an amazing woman whom everyone loved.

Frances Elizabeth Eshelman passed away on December 26, 2011, several weeks after taking a fall and breaking her hip. God bless her sweet soul, as we have been blessed by her presence here in our life. May her memory live on through this book and through other works which she has inspired.

This bookcover is a photocopy of the original bookcover, which was made by Dr. Evans and her 96 year old mother, Frances Eshelman, from pictures of flowers cut from catalogs and glued onto cardboard cut from a cereal box. Creativity is one of God's best healing gifts!

www.ingramcontent.com/pod-product-compliance
Lightning Source LLC
LaVergne TN
LVHW010025070426
835509LV00001B/5